Meditations
to
Heal Your
Life

Also by Louise L. Hay

Meditations to
Heal Your Life

Gift Edition

Louise L. Hay

Hay House, Inc.
Carlsbad, California • Sydney, Australia
Canada • Hong Kong • United Kingdom

Published and distributed in the United States by:
    Hay House, Inc., P.O. Box 5100, Carlsbad, CA 92018-5100
(800) 654-5126 • (800) 650-5115 (fax) • www.hayhouse.com
    Hay House Australia Pty Ltd, P.O. Box 515, Brighton-Le-Sands NSW 2216
phone: 1800 023 516 • *e-mail:* info@hayhouse.com.au

Editorial supervision: Jill Kramer
Interior design: Summer McStravick
Illustrations: © 2002 Joan Perrin Falquet

Library of Congress Cataloging-in-Publication Data

Hay, Louise L.
    Meditations to heal your life / Louise L. Hay.— Gift ed.
        p. cm.
    ISBN 1-56170-995-6
    1. Meditations. 2. Affirmations. 3. Mental healing. I. Title.
    BL624.2 .H38 2002
    291.4'32—dc21

                                                            2002000761

                    ISBN 1-56170-995-6

                05 04 03 02   4 3 2 1
                1st printing, August 2002

            Printed in China by Palace Press

To all students on the pathway of Life

who realize the importance of

learning to love themselves,

I dedicate this book to all of us.

CONTENTS

INTRODUCTION

*T*his is a book of ideas to spark your own creative thinking process. It will give you an opportunity to see other ways to approach your experiences.

We come into this world with such pure, clear minds, totally connected with our inner wisdom. As we grow, we pick up fears and limitations from the adults around us. By the time we reach adulthood, we have a lot of negative beliefs that we're not even aware of. And we tend to build our lives and our experiences upon those false beliefs.

As you read this book, you may find statements that you don't agree with; they may clash with your own belief systems. That's all right. It's what I call "stirring up the pot." You don't have to agree with everything I say. But please examine what you believe and why. This is how you'll grow and change.

When I first started out on my pathway, I used to challenge many of the metaphysical concepts I heard. The more I examined my own beliefs in relation to the new ideas, the more I realized that I believed many things that were contributing to the unhappiness in my life. As I began to release the old, negative concepts, my life also changed for the better.

Begin reading anywhere in this book. Open it at will. The message will be perfect for you at that moment. It may confirm what you already believe, or it may challenge you. It's all part of the growth process. Know that you are safe and all is well.

Louise L. Hay

I choose to dwell
in a world of
love and acceptance

ACCEPTANCE

Life is sacred. I hold in my heart all the parts of my-self—the infant, the child, the teenager, the young adult, the adult, and my present and future self. Every embarrassment, mistake, hurt, and wound, I accept fully as part of my story. My story includes every success and every failure, every error and every truthful insight, and all of it is valuable in ways I do not have to completely understand. In this moment in time, I choose to accept and love every part of myself. I have compassion for me, and I also feel compassion for others. I create a life of acceptance and understanding.

I radiate acceptance.

I claim my

power and move

beyond all

limitations.

ADDICTION

Heavy dependence on anything outside myself is called an "addiction." I can be addicted to drugs and alcohol, to sex and tobacco; and I can also be addicted to blaming or judging people, to illness, to debt, to being a victim, and to being rejected. Yet, I can move beyond these limitations. Being addicted is giving up my power to a substance or a habit. I can always take my power back. *This is the moment I take my power back!* I choose to develop the positive habit of knowing that Life is here for me. I am willing to forgive myself and move on. I have an eternal spirit that has always been with me, and it is here with me now. I relax and let go, and I remember to breathe as I release old habits and practice positive ones.

*I forgive myself,
and I set myself free.*

I use my
affirmations
wisely.

AFFIRMATIONS

Every single thought I have and every sentence I speak is an affirmation. It is either positive or negative. Positive affirmations create positive experiences, and negative affirmations create negative experiences. If I continually repeat negative statements about myself or about life, I only keep producing more negative experiences. I now rise beyond my old habit of seeing life in a negative way. My new affirmation habit is to only speak of the good I want in my life. Then, only good will come to me.

In the Beginning is the Word.

I choose

the thoughts

that make me

feel comfortable

with growing older.

AGING

Each year is special and precious and filled with wonders all its own. Being elderly is as special as being a child. Yet, our culture fears old age so much. We have made it such a terrible, terrible thing to get old. And yet it is normal and natural. The youth-worship culture is harmful to us all. I choose to look forward to growing older. The alternative is to leave the planet. I choose to love myself at every age. Just because I am older, it does not mean I have to get sick and infirm. I do not have to be hooked up to machines or suffer in a nursing home in order to leave the planet. When it is my time to go, I will do it gently—perhaps I will go to bed, take a nap, and leave peacefully. In the meantime, I continue to enjoy each day.

I am always the perfect age.

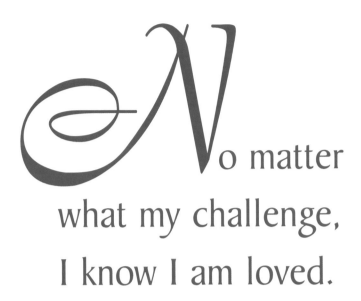

*N*o matter
what my challenge,
I know I am loved.

We are walking through uncharted waters here. And everyone involved is doing the best they can with the knowledge and understanding that they have at this point in time and space. I am proud of myself for doing more than I thought I could. Someone, somewhere, on this planet has been healed of every single dis-case that we have been able to create. There has to be a healing answer. It does not matter what language I speak. Love speaks to us all from the heart. I spend time every day just quieting down and feeling the love from my heart go through my arms and legs and through every organ in my body. Love is a healing power. Love opens all doors. Love is an ever-ready Universal Power that is here to help me overcome every challenge in my life. I open my heart. I let the love flow. I feel Oneness with the Power that created me.

This, too, shall pass, and we will grow and benefit from it.

I am the main authority in my world.

AUTHORITY

*N*o person, place, or thing has any power over me, for I am the only thinker in my mind. As a child, I accepted authority figures as gods. Now I am learning to take back my power and become my own authority figure. I accept myself as a powerful, responsible being. As I meditate every morning, I get in touch with my own inner wisdom. The school of life is deeply fulfilling as I come to know that we are all students and all teachers. We each have come to learn something and to teach something. As I listen to my thoughts, I gently guide my mind toward trusting my own Inner Wisdom. I grow and blossom and entrust all my affairs on Earth to the Divine Source. All is well.

I am the author
of my life.

 go beyond

barriers to possibilities.

BARRIERS

The gateways to wisdom and learning are always open, and more and more, I am choosing to walk through them. Barriers, blocks, obstacles, and problems are personal teachers giving me the opportunity to move out of the past and into the Totality of Possibilities. I love stretching my mind, thinking of the highest good imaginable. As my mind can conceive of more good, the barriers and blocks dissolve. My life becomes full of little miracles popping up out of the blue. And every now and then, I give myself permission to do absolutely nothing but sit and be open to Divine Wisdom. I am a student of life, and I love it.

All of the barriers in my life are dissolving.

I find beauty in
everything in my world.

BEAUTY

Beauty is everywhere. Natural beauty shines forth from every little flower, from the patterns of reflected light on the surface of water, from the quiet strength of old trees. Nature thrills me; it renews and refreshes me. I find relaxation, enjoyment, and healing in the simplest things in life. As I look with love at nature, I find it easy to look with love at myself. I am part of nature; thus, I am beautiful in my own unique way. Wherever I look, I see beauty. Today I resonate with all the beauty in life.

Beauty arouses
and heals me.

$\mathcal{M}$y bills are

an affirmation of my

ability to pay.

BILLS

The Power that created me has put everything here for me. It is up to me to deserve and to accept. Whatever I have now is what I have accepted. If I want something different, something more, or something less, I do not get it by complaining. I can only get something else by expanding my consciousness. I welcome all my bills with love, and I rejoice as I write out the checks, knowing that what I am sending out is coming back to me multiplied. I feel positive about this issue. Bills are really wonderful things. It means that somebody has trusted me enough to give me their service or product, knowing that I have the ability to pay for it.

I pay my way easily.

17

I trust Divine Intelligence to influence my business, and I go from success to success.

I trust Divine Intelligence to run my business. Whether I own my own business in a worldly sense or not, I am an instrument employed by this Divine Intelligence. There is only One Intelligence, and It has a splendid track record in the history of our solar system, guiding each of the planets for millions of years along pathways that are orderly and harmonious. I willingly accept this Intelligence as my Partner in business. It is easy for me to channel my energy into working with this Powerful Intelligence. Out of this Intelligence comes all the answers, all the solutions, all the healing, and all the new creations and ideas that make my business such a joyous success.

My business is doing what I love.

I take care of
myself the best
I can.

CAREGIVERS

*M*y body is a miracle. The bodies of the people I care for are also miracles. Our bodies know how to handle emergencies, and they know how to rest and replenish themselves. We are all learning to listen to our bodies and to give our bodies what they need. Sometimes caring for others is an overwhelming job. It is more than we had anticipated. I learn to ask for help. Whether I am a caregiver or a care-receiver, loving myself is one of the most important things I can do. When I truly love and accept myself exactly as I am, it is as though I shift gears on some level. Suddenly I can relax and know, deep in my heart, that all is well.

I am a shining light.

$\mathcal{I}$ change
my thinking
with love.

My New Beliefs

CHANGING MY THINKING

J am Light. I am Spirit. I am a wonderful, capable being. And it is time for me to acknowledge that I create my own reality with my thoughts. If I want to change my reality, then it is time for me to change my mind. I do this by choosing to think and speak in new and positive ways. I learned a long time ago that if I would change my thinking, I could change my life. Changing my thinking is really dropping my limitations. As I do so, I begin to be aware of the infinity of life all around me. I begin to understand that I am already perfect, whole, and complete. Each day gets better!

I change my life when
I change my thinking.

o matter what happened in the past, I now begin to allow the tiny child inside to blossom, and to know that it is deeply loved.

CHILD ABUSE

We are all beloved children of the Universe, and yet there are dreadful things happening to us, such as child abuse. It is said that 30 percent of our population has experienced child abuse. This is not something new. We are at a point right now where we are beginning to allow ourselves to be aware of things that we used to conceal behind walls of silence. These walls are starting to come down so that we can make changes. Awareness is the first step in making those changes. For those of us who had really difficult childhoods, our walls and armors are very thick and strong. Still, behind our walls, the little child in each one of us just wants to be noticed and loved and accepted exactly as is—not changed or made different. I love you, little one.

It is safe for me to grow up.

I can teach,

but I cannot force.

CHILDREN

*O*pen, loving communication with children is one of my greatest joys. I listen to what they say, and they listen to what I say. Children always imitate adults, so if a child near me is behaving negatively, I examine my own negative beliefs. I know that as I heal myself, I will also help to heal the child. I affirm that I love myself unconditionally. I become consciously willing to let go of all negative beliefs. I become an example of a positive, loving person. The child can then begin to love herself or himself, and their negative behavior dissolves, sometimes immediately, sometimes gradually. I also connect with my own inner child. As I stabilize my adult life, my inner child feels safe and loved . . . and with safety and love comes the willingness to go beyond many old patterns.

I love children,
and they love me.

I choose to move beyond where I was when I got up this morning . . . and open myself up to something new.

CHOICE

I choose to remember that every problem has a solution. And to know that this, too, is something I can deal with. Because I choose to look at a situation in this way, the present problem is a temporary thing to me. It is something that I am working through. I am a good person. I choose to let go of feeling sorry for myself. I am willing to learn the lesson and to open up to the good that the Universe has to offer. I choose to be willing to change. I accept the fact that I will not always know how things are to be worked out. I can trust and I can know. Everything is working out for the best. All is well.

I choose to live my highest awareness.

I communicate with love . . . and attract loving experiences and people to me.

*L*oving communication is one of the happiest and most powerful experiences for people. How do I get to this space? I have done a lot of work on myself. I have read many books, and I have come to understand the principles of life, such as, "What I think and say goes out *from* me, the Universe responds, and it comes back *to* me." So I begin to ask for help and to observe myself. As I allow myself the space to watch without judgment and without criticism, I begin to make great progress in loving communication. What do I believe? What do I feel? How do I react? How can I love more? And then I say to the Universe, "Teach me to love."

Communication is a song of love.

The community of human beings on Planet Earth is opening up on a scale that has never been seen before. New levels of spirituality are connecting us. We are learning, on a soul level, that we are all one. I have chosen to incarnate at this time for a reason. I believe we have chosen on a deep level to be a part of the healing process of the planet. I remember that every time I think a thought, it goes out from me and connects with like-minded people who are thinking the same thing. I cannot move to new levels of consciousness if I remain stuck in old judgments, prejudices, guilt, and fear. As I practice Unconditional Love with respect to myself and others, the entire planet begins to heal.

I open my heart to all of the beings on the planet.

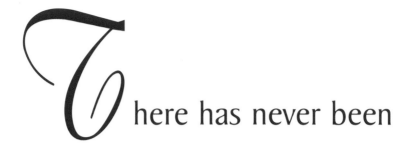
here has never been another person like me since time began, so there is nothing and no one to compare or compete with.

COMPARISONS

I am here to learn to love myself and to love other people unconditionally. Even though every person has measurable things about them, such as height and weight, there is far more to me than my physical expression. This immeasurable part of me is where my power is. Comparing myself with others makes me feel either superior or inferior, never acceptable exactly as I am. What a waste of time and energy! We are all unique, wonderful beings, each different and special. I go within and connect with the unique expression of eternal Oneness that I am and we all are. Everything in the physical world changes. As I flow with these changes, I keep relating to that inside me, which is deeper than any change.

I am incomparable.

*W*hat I see in
my world is a mirror
of what I have
in my mind.

CONSCIOUSNESS

I am Pure Consciousness. I can use this Consciousness in any way I desire. I can choose to be conscious of the realm of lack and limitation, or I can choose to be conscious of the realm of Infinite Oneness, Harmony, and Wholeness. It is One Infinite Consciousness viewed either negatively or positively. At all times I am one with all of life, and I am free to experience love, harmony, beauty, strength, joy, and so much more. I am Consciousness. I am energy. I am safe. I keep learning and growing and changing my consciousness and changing my experience. All is well.

My power comes through the use of my mind.

The only thing I ever control is my current thinking. My current thought, the one I am thinking now, is totally under my control.

CONTROL

*I*f something happens that I feel I have no control over, then I affirm a positive statement immediately. I keep saying it over and over to myself until I move through that little space. When things don't feel right, I might say this to myself: *All is well, all is well, all is well.* Whenever I feel the urge to control things, I say, *I trust the process of life.* During earthquakes or other natural disasters, I say to myself, *I am in rhythm and harmony with the earth and the movement of the earth.* In this way, whatever happens is okay because I am in harmony with the flow of life.

I create my own security by trusting the process of life.

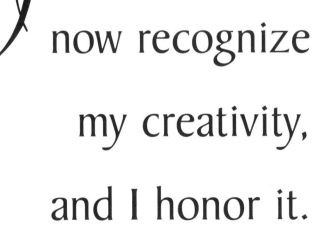

I now recognize
my creativity,
and I honor it.

CREATIVITY

The creativity of the Universe flows through me all day long, and all I have to do to participate in it is know that I am a part of it. It is easy to recognize creativity when it comes in the form of a painting, a novel, a movie, a new wine, or a new business. Yet I am creating my entire life every moment from the most common, ordinary creation of new cells in my body—from choosing my emotional responses, to my present job, to my bank account, to my relationships with friends, and to my very attitudes about myself. One of my most powerful gifts is my imagination. I use it to see good things happening to me and to everyone around me. I am peaceful as I co-create my life with my Higher Self.

*I create my
life each day.*

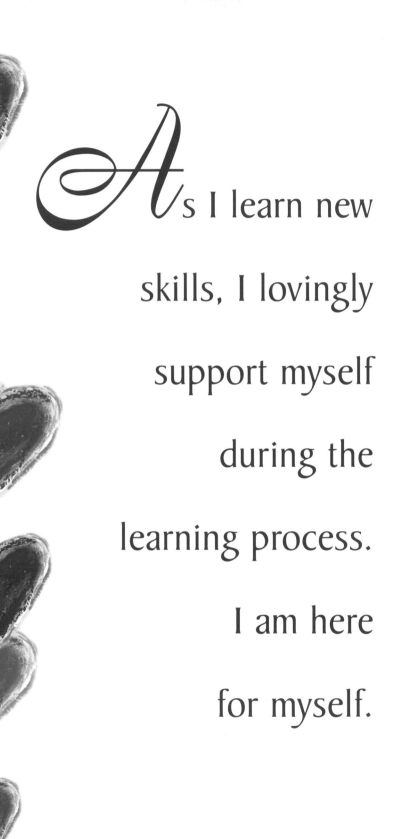

As I learn new skills, I lovingly support myself during the learning process. I am here for myself.

CRITICISM

I am a wonderful being. I used to scold and criticize myself because I believed it would help me improve my life, yet criticism has not improved me over the years. In fact, criticism seems to make it harder to change and progress. So, as I listen to my inner dialogue and find that I am being critical, telling myself that I am not good enough or that I am doing something wrong, I recognize the old patterns of childhood, and I immediately begin to speak lovingly to my inner child. Instead of tearing myself apart, I choose to nourish myself with praise and approval. I know I am on the way to becoming consistently loving.

I praise myself for big and little things.

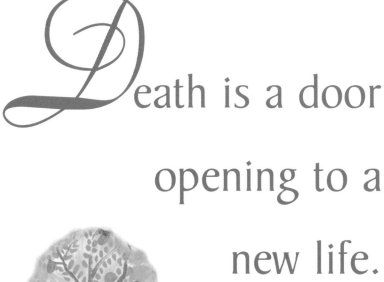

Death is a door
opening to a
new life.

DEATH

$\mathcal{I}$ came in during the middle of the movie . . . and I will leave in the middle of the movie. There is no right time or wrong time, just *my* time. Death is not a failure. Vegetarians die and meat eaters die. People who curse die and people who meditate die. Good people die, and not-so-good people die. Everybody passes. It is a normal and natural process. As one door to life closes, another one opens. As the door to this life closes, the door to my next life opens. The love I take with me greets me in my next experience. Death is a releasing method of being born into the next phase of everlasting, eternal life. I know that no matter where I am, I am always safe and loved and totally supported by Life.

I am at peace with my life . . . and my death.

I decide to

go beyond my

present limited

human-mind

thinking.

Yes, I can.

46

DECISION MAKING

When I care about my physical well-being, I select healthy, nutritious foods to eat. When I care about my mental and emotional well-being, I decide to choose thoughts that create a solid inner foundation for myself. One idle thought does not mean very much, but thoughts that I think over and over are like drops of water: First there is a puddle, then a pond, then a lake, then an ocean. Repeated criticism and thoughts of lack and limitation drown my consciousness in a sea of negativity, while repeated thoughts of Truth and peace and love lift me up so that I float on the ocean of life with ease. Thoughts that connect me with the Oneness of life make it easier for me to make good decisions and stick to them.

I am a decisive person.

DESERVING

*A*ll people deserve happy, fulfilling lives. Like most people, I used to believe that I deserved only a little bit of good. Few people believe they deserve *all good!* There is no need to limit our good. Most of us have been conditioned to believe that the good in life can only be had if you eat your spinach, clean your room, comb your hair, shine your shoes, keep quiet, and so on. Although these may be important things to learn, they have nothing to do with inner self-worth. I know that I am already good enough, and that without changing anything at all, I deserve a wonderful life. I open my arms wide and declare with love that I deserve and accept *all* good.

I am open to the most splendid experiences.

I assimilate the good

in life and

make it

true for me.

DIGESTION

I assimilate, digest, and eliminate life perfectly. My cells and organs know exactly what to do, and I help them do *their* job by doing *my* job of eating nutritious food and thinking clear, positive, loving thoughts. For every part of my body, there is a mental pattern: The stomach is the part of me where ideas are digested and assimilated. When new experiences happen, I sometimes have problems assimilating them. And yet, even in the midst of a big change, I can always choose the thoughts that glorify my most essential and eternal being. I am a Divine, magnificent expression of Life.

I digest life with ease.

$\mathcal{I}$ lovingly

create perfect health

for myself.

DIS-EASE

It is natural that I am healthy, and it is natural that I am flexible. I am able to learn new things easily—to laugh, to change, and to grow. Dis-ease is related to a resistance to flowing with life in some area, and to the inability to forgive. I look at dis-ease as if it is a personal teacher that comes to help me on my pathway to greater understanding. Like all teachers, it is a stepping-stone, and when I learn the lesson, I move on to the next phase of my healing. Every person on the planet is involved in healing their life in some area. I help my body, my mind, and my spirit live healthfully by creating a loving atmosphere around myself. It is my body and my mind, and I am in charge.

Any dis-ease I have is a valuable teacher.

When I meditate,

I sit down and ask,

"What is it I need to know?"

At some point

during the day,

I get an

answer.

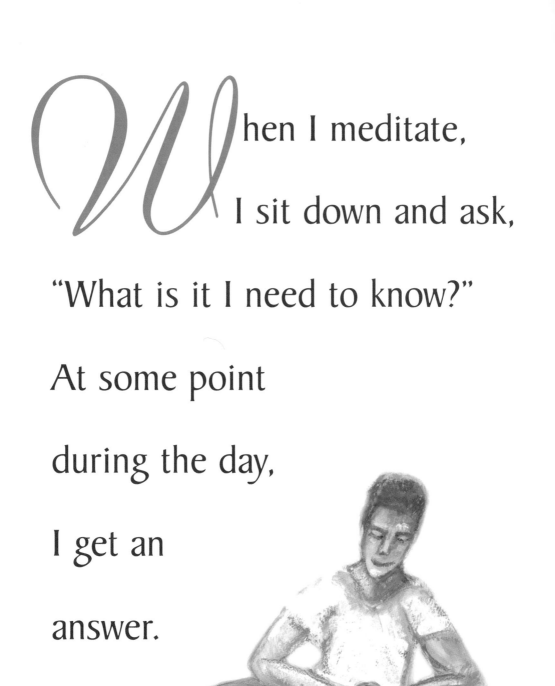

DIVINE GUIDANCE

I know that there is a Power far greater than myself that flows through me every moment of every day, and I can open myself to this Power and receive what I need, whenever I choose. This is true for everyone. We are all learning that it is safe to look within. It is safe to enlarge my viewpoint of life. If things are not going the way I expected in some area, it does not mean that I am bad or wrong. It is a signal that I am being redirected by Divine Guidance. When this happens, I find a quiet place where I can relax and connect with the Intelligence within me. I affirm that the supply of wisdom is inexhaustible and available to me, and that whatever I need to know is revealed to me in the perfect time/space sequence.

All is in Divine right order.

I feel

good about

what I do.

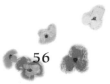

DOING

I flow with an attitude of serendipity through all kinds of experiences. There are endless ways of doing things. If I have done a great deal of work, I rejoice. If I have done very little work, I rejoice. If I have done nothing at all, I still rejoice. Whatever I do is perfect in the moment. There is really nothing that I "have to do." There are things that might be best to do; however, I always have a choice. Life is an adventure, and the Universe is always on my side!

I flow with life easily and effortlessly.

$\mathcal{M}$y dreams

are a joyful,

loving

experience.

DREAMS

I do not listen to or watch the news before I go to sleep at night. The news is often a list of disasters, and I do not want to take that into my dream state. Much clearing work is done in dreams. I can also ask my dreams for help with anything I am working on. I will often find an answer by morning. I prepare myself for sleep by doing something special that helps me calm down. I might use these affirmations: *Every corner of my world is a safe place. Even in the dark of night when I sleep, I am safe. I know that tomorrow will take care of itself. My dreams are dreams of joy. I love waking up.* Silently, while still under the covers, I give thanks for my cozy bed and all my many blessings. And if I awaken with a dream, I ask it to tell me about itself. Daily practice of my mental skills can begin before I even open my eyes.

My bed is a safe place.

I am a skilled driver

and a friendly passenger.

DRIVING MY CAR

*D*riving is a safe and pleasant experience for me. I take good care of my car, and my car takes good care of me. It is ready to go whenever I am. I have the perfect mechanic, who also loves my car. I fill my car with love whenever I enter it, so love is always traveling with me. I send love to the other drivers on the road, as we are all traveling together. Love goes before me, and love greets me at my destination. I am always safe and Divinely protected.

I love my car.

$\mathcal{I}$ love
and experience
every age.

ELDER YEARS

*I*n the early part of the last century, life expectancy was 49 years. Today, it is about 85. Tomorrow it could be 125. It is time for us to change the way we view our later years. No longer will I accept the notion that I must become sick and die lonely and afraid. It is time to make nursing homes obsolete as I learn to take responsibility for my own health. I take control of my thoughts, and I create an elder time that is far grander than any other generation's. I see myself as vital, vivacious, healthy, fully alive, and contributing until my last day. As I move into my treasure years, I allow myself to become an Elder of Excellence. I lead the way in also showing others how to be fully alive at every age. I have the ability to contribute to our society and to make the world a better place for the next generation.

I rejoice in each passing year.

It is okay to make a good income without working hard.

EMPLOYMENT

As I employ my Higher Self, my Higher Self employs me. What a wonderful, brilliant, delicate, strong, beautiful energy my inner spirit is. It blesses me with fulfilling work. Each day is new and different. As I let go of the struggle to survive, I find that I am fed, clothed, housed, and loved in ways that are deeply fulfilling to me. I make it okay for myself and others to have money without working hard at a job. I am worthy of bringing in good money without struggling in the rat race or fighting traffic. I follow my higher instincts and listen to my heart in all that I do.

I employ positive thoughts.

$\mathcal{L}$oving myself gives me the extra energy needed to work through any problem more quickly.

ENERGY

I liberate my energy by doing things that delight me. As I consciously acknowledge the energy of love in my life, I dissolve old grudges that wear me down. When I feel tired, I rest. I even give myself permission to do absolutely nothing every once in a while. My energy is radiant and peaceful today. Laughing, singing, and dancing are my natural, normal, spontaneous expressions. I know that I am part of the Divine plan. I am creating space inside myself for loving, optimistic, and cheerful patterns to constantly germinate, take root, and grow. I nourish them with my positive attitudes.

I am filled with positive energy.

$\mathcal{I}$ am open

and receptive to

all the good

in the

Universe.

ENLIGHTENMENT

Awakening to love is what I am doing each morning. I love stretching my mind and acting as if I am already perfect, whole, and complete, right here and right now. My heart is open and receptive to all good as I let go of striving and straining to get what I need. I know that everything I need and desire comes to me in the perfect time/space sequence. I feel peaceful knowing that the Universe is on my side. As I align my consciousness with my Higher Self, I flow with an attitude of serendipity through all kinds of experiences.

Enlightenment is my 24-hour-a-day job.

 bless others'

good fortune, and

I know that there is

plenty for all.

My consciousness determines my prosperity. The One Infinite Intelligence always says yes to me, and I say yes to all good. Reverend Ike, the well-known New York City evangelist, remembers walking by fine restaurants and lovely homes and fancy automobiles when he was a poor preacher, and saying out loud, *"That's for me, that's for me."* I rejoice out loud when I see abundance, and I mentally make room for it to come into my life. Being grateful for what I have helps to increase it. This also works with talents and abilities and good health. I recognize prosperity everywhere and rejoice in it!

Other people's prosperity mirrors my own abundance.

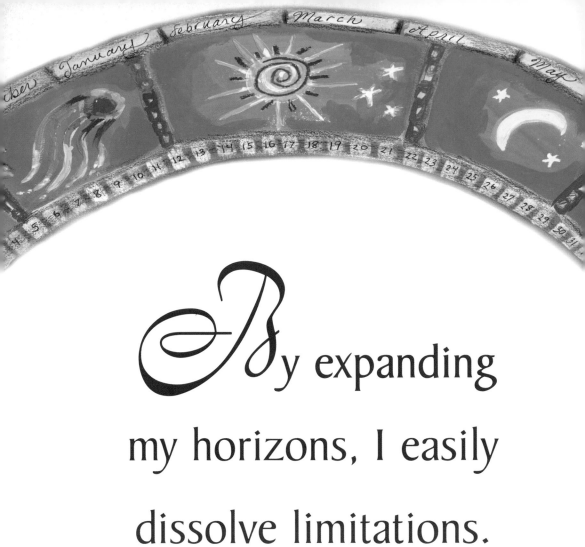

$\mathscr{B}$y expanding my horizons, I easily dissolve limitations.

EXPANDING HORIZONS

*L*ife really is free and easy. It is my thinking that is difficult, limited, shame-based, or not good enough. If I open myself to unlearning some of my limited thinking patterns and learning something new, then I can grow and change. Or do I already know it all? The trouble with knowing it all is that I don't get to grow, and nothing new can come in. Do I really accept that there's a Power and an Intelligence greater than I am? Or do I think I'm the whole thing? If I think I'm *it*, then of course I'm frightened. If I realize that there's a Power and an Intelligence in this Universe far greater and brighter than I am, and which is on my side, then I can move into that mental space where life can operate freely and easily.

Life is free and easy.

*U*nconditional love is really just love without expectations.

EXPECTATIONS

I love myself in this present moment exactly as I am. As I do this, I feel my stomach relax, and I feel the muscles in my neck and back adjust themselves gently. I used to resist loving and accepting myself, believing that I had to wait until I lost the weight or got the job, the lover, the money, or whatever. What happened was that when I lost the weight or got the money, I still didn't love myself, and I just made another list. Today, I drop my list of expectations! This moment is incredibly powerful. I am enjoying the feeling of just letting myself be who I am.

I can just be who I am.

$\mathcal{I}$ picked the perfect family for this lifetime.

FAMILY

I envelop my entire family in a circle of love—those who are living and those who are dead. I affirm wonderful, harmonious experiences that are meaningful for all of us. I feel so blessed to be part of the timeless web of unconditional love that brings us all together. Ancestors who lived before me did the best they could with the knowledge and understanding they had, and children not yet born will face new challenges and will do the best they can with the knowledge and understanding *they* will have. Each day I see my task more clearly, which is to simply let go of old family limitations and awaken to Divine harmony. For me, family get-togethers are opportunities to practice tolerance and compassion.

All living beings are part of my family.

FEAR

At any moment, I have the opportunity of choosing love or fear. In moments of fear, I remember the sun: It is always shining, even though clouds may obscure it for a while. Like the sun, the One Infinite Power is eternally shining its Light upon me, even though clouds of negative thinking may temporarily obscure it. I choose to remember the Light. I feel secure in the Light. And when the fears come, I choose to see them as passing clouds in the sky, and I let them go on their way. I am not my fears. It is safe for me to live without guarding and defending myself all the time. I know that what we do in our hearts is very important, so I begin every day in a silent connection with my heart. When I feel afraid, I open my heart and let the love dissolve the fear.

I am safe.

 cannot be lost

or lonely or abandoned,

for I dwell in

Divine Intelligence.

FEELING LOST

When I feel lost, or when something I need is lost, I stop my panicky thoughts and drop into the Intelligence within me that knows that nothing is ever lost in Divine Mind. This Intelligence is everywhere. It is in everything around me. It is in what I am looking for, and is within me here and now. I affirm that this One Intelligence is now bringing me what I am looking for together in the perfect time/space sequence. I am never stuck. Several times throughout the day, I let go of my limiting identities and remind myself of who I really am— a Divine, magnificent expression of life, created by a loving and infinite Intelligence. All is well.

There is only one Intelligence.

I create my own feelings through the thoughts I choose to think. I have the ability to make different choices and create different experiences.

FEELINGS

I can heal what I can feel, so I must allow myself to feel my feelings. So many people put judgments on their feelings. They feel they "should not" be angry, but they are. They are searching for a way to deal with their feelings. There are many safe ways to express feelings: I can beat pillows, scream in the car, run, or play tennis. I can have a heated conversation in front of a mirror with the people I am angry at or hurt by or afraid of. I imagine these people standing before me. I look in the mirror and tell them how I really feel. I get it all out, and then finish with something such as, "Okay, that is done, I release you and let you go. Now, what do I believe about myself that created this? And what belief could I change so that I will not react with anger all the time?" This is an incredible time to be alive. I am gentle with myself as I learn my lessons and move through life.

Feelings are thoughts in motion in my body.

I am

financially

comfortable.

FINANCES

I allow my income to constantly expand, no matter what the newspapers and economists say. I move beyond my present income, and I go beyond the economic forecasts. I do not listen to people out there telling me how far I can go or what I can do. I easily go beyond my parents' income level. My consciousness of finances is constantly expanding and taking in new ideas—new ways to live deeply, richly, comfortably, and beautifully. My talents and abilities are more than good enough, and it is deeply pleasurable for me to share them with the world. I go beyond any feelings that I do not deserve, and I move into acceptance of an entirely new level of financial security.

Financial security is a constant in my life.

$\mathcal{L}$ove is all I need

to fix my world.

FIXING IT

*E*very day it gets easier to look into my own eyes in the mirror and say, "I love you just the way you are." My life improves without my fixing it up. I used to be a fix-it person: I would fix my relationships; I would fix my bank account; I would fix things with my boss, my health, and my creativity. Then one day, I discovered magic. If I could really love myself, really love every part of myself, incredible miracles would occur in my life. My problems would seem to dissolve, and there would be nothing to fix. So the focus of my attention had changed from fixing problems to loving myself and trusting the Universe to bring me everything I need and everything I desire.

Loving myself is my magic wand.

$\mathcal{F}$ood is a good friend. I thank it for nourishing me.

F O O D

Eating good, nutritious food is deeply pleasurable whether I am at home, in a restaurant, camping, hiking, or taking my lunch break at the office. I love myself; therefore, I choose to be aware of what I put in my mouth and how it makes me feel. When I eat, I am putting fuel into my body to give me energy. Every body is different, so I find the kind of fuel that *my* body needs to have optimum health and energy. Fast foods can be fun occasionally, but there are many people who feel it is normal to exist on sodas, cakes, and processed convenience foods that have little nutrition in them. Learning about the basics of good nutrition is fun and energizing. I enjoy cooking and eating delicious, healthful, natural food.

I feel energized and happy when I eat well.

Forgiveness

is the healing

tool I carry

with me

everywhere.

FORGIVENESS

I love the feeling of freedom I get when I take off my heavy coat of criticism, fear, guilt, resentment, and shame. I can then forgive myself and others. This sets us all free. I am willing to give up my "stuff" around old issues. I refuse to live in the past any longer. I forgive myself for having carried those old burdens for so long. I forgive myself for not knowing how to love myself and others. Each person is responsible for their own behavior, and what they give out, life will give back to them. So I have no need to punish anyone. We are all under the laws of our own consciousness, myself included. I go about my own business of clearing out the un-forgiving parts of my mind, and I allow the love to come in. Then I am healed.

I am willing to forgive.

I make new,

more supportive

choices.

FREEDOM TO CHOOSE

*N*o person, place, or thing has any power over me unless I give it, for I am the only thinker in my mind. I have immense freedom in that I can choose what to think. I can choose to see life in positive ways instead of complaining or being mad at myself or other people. Complaining about what I do not have is one way to handle a situation, but it does not change anything. When I love myself and find myself in the midst of a negative situation, I can say something such as, "I am willing to release the pattern in my consciousness that contributed to this condition." I have made negative choices in the past, but this does not mean that I am a bad person, nor am I stuck with these negative choices. I can always choose to let go of the old judgments.

I always have the freedom to choose my thoughts.

*A*ppreciation and acceptance act like power-ful magnets for miracles every moment of the day. If somebody compliments me, I smile and say thank you. Compliments are gifts of prosperity. I have learned to accept them graciously. Today is a sacred gift from Life. I open my arms wide to receive the full measure of prosperity that the Universe offers this day. Any time of the day or night, I can let it in. I know that there are times in life when the Universe gives to me, and I am not in a position to do anything about giving back. I can think of many people who really helped me so much at a time when there was no way I could ever repay them. Later, I have been able to help others, and that is the way life goes. I relax and rejoice in the abundance that is here right now.

I give and receive gifts graciously.

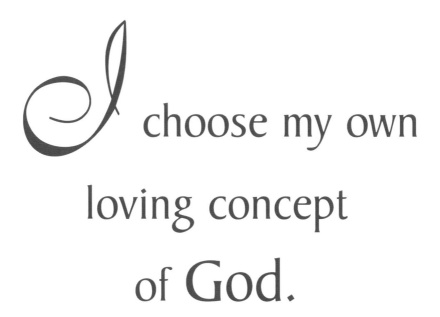

I choose my own
loving concept
of **God**.

GOD

I have the power to choose to see things as they really are. I choose to see things as God does, with the eyes of love. Since it is the nature of God to be present everywhere, to be all-powerful and all-knowing, I know that all there really is in this entire Universe is the love of God. The love of God surrounds me, dwells within me, goes before me, and smooths the way for me. I am a Beloved Child of the Universe, and the Universe lovingly takes care of me now and forevermore. When I need something, I turn to the Power that created me. I ask for what I need, and then I give thanks even before receiving, knowing that it will come to me in the perfect time/space sequence.

One Power created us all.

I share only the good news.

GOSSIP

Once I became aware of the harm that gossip does to everyone involved with it, I decided to stop gossiping completely. So I have learned that it is best if I speak well of my companions. Then, by the law of life, they also speak well of me. In this way, good vibrations accompany me and greet me wherever I go. I like taking the time to be considerate of others, and I absolutely relish communicating in a way that uplifts and inspires people. Knowing that what we give out comes back to us, I carefully choose the words I use. If I hear a negative story, I do not repeat it. If I hear a positive story, I tell everyone.

I am an excellent communicator.

$\mathcal{I}$ accept my

loved one's

passing.

GRIEVING

The mourning process takes at least a year. I give myself time and space to go through this natural, normal process of life. I am gentle with myself. I allow myself to go through the grief in my own way. It takes a full year before it begins to dissipate. I have to experience the special holidays I shared with my loved one. I am aware that I can never lose anyone because I have never owned anyone. And in what will seem like the twinkling of an eye, I will connect with that soul again. I know that everybody dies, including me. Trees, animals, birds, rivers, and even stars are born and die. And it is all in the perfect time/space sequence. All truly is well.

I am at peace with the grieving process.

 value my

freedom, so I neither

give nor receive guilt.

GUILT

As a child, I was manipulated through guilt into good behavior: "Don't be like that. Don't say that. No, no, no!" Religion also uses guilt to keep people in line, even telling them that they will burn in hell if they "misbehave." I forgive the churches and church authorities. I choose to forgive my parents and to forgive myself. Many of us have been living under a very heavy mantle of guilt, feeling "not good enough" for whatever reason. This is a new day. I take back my power! I start by loving and accepting myself unconditionally.

I love and accept myself exactly as I am.

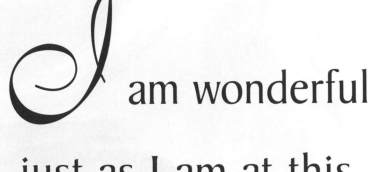

I am wonderful just as I am at this very moment.

HEADACHES

One of the mental patterns that con-
tributes to headaches is the need to
make ourselves wrong. The next time I get a
headache, I will ask myself, "How am I making
myself wrong? What have I just done that I am
putting myself down for?" I have learned to listen to my inner dialogue, and when negative
thoughts pass through my mind, telling me that
I am not good enough or that I am doing something wrong, I recognize the old patterns of childhood, and I begin to speak lovingly to myself
and my inner child. Instead of tearing myself
down with critical thinking, I choose to build
myself up with loving thoughts of approval. If I
become aware of something that is pressuring me,
I look for ways to handle that pressure differently.
I approve of myself.

*I approve of what I
see in myself.*

My body is
balanced, healthy, and
happy . . . and so am I.

HEALING

I am open and receptive to all the healing energies in the Universe. I know that every cell in my body is intelligent and knows how to heal itself. My body is always working toward perfect health. I now release any and all impediments to my perfect healing. I learn about nutrition and feed my body nourishing, wholesome food. I watch my thinking and only think healthy thoughts. I release, wipe out, and eliminate all thoughts of hatred, jealousy, anger, fear, self-pity, shame, and guilt. I love my body. I send love to each organ, bone, muscle, and part of my body. I flood the cells of my body with love. I am grateful to my body for all the good health I have had in the past. I accept healing and good health here and now.

Good health is my Divine right.

Loving myself and others allows me to be all that I can be.

HIGHEST GOOD

The Power that created me is the same Power that I co-create with, and this Power only wants me to express and experience my highest good. I do my best to make my real self vitally important and give it control of everything. By doing this, I am truly loving my self. It opens me to greater possibilities, to freedom, joy, and unpredictably wonderful daily miracles. My highest good includes the highest good for others, too. This is truly a loving act.

I always work for my highest good.

$\mathcal{H}$olidays are

happy

times for me.

HOLIDAYS

*R*eligious and civil holidays are times to celebrate with friends and reflect upon the processes of life. I follow my inner voice through each holiday, always knowing that I am in the right place at the right time, doing the right thing for me. I have fun at parties and holiday get-togethers. I know how to have a good time *and* be responsible and safe, all in the same evening. There is time for laughter and time for being grateful for my many blessings. I connect with my inner child, and we do something together, just the two of us. When I go shopping for holiday gifts, I easily purchase what I need at prices I can afford. Everyone welcomes the gifts I give.

Every day is a holy day.

My inner home

and my outer home

are places of beauty

and tranquility.

HOME

$\mathcal{I}$ am at home in my own heart. I take my heart with me wherever I live. As I begin to love myself, I find myself providing a safe and comfortable home for myself. I begin to feel at home in my own body. My home is a reflection of my mind and what I feel I am worthy of. If my home is a disaster zone and I feel overwhelmed, then I begin cleaning in one corner of one of the rooms. Just like with my mind: I begin with changing one thought at a time. Eventually, the entire place will be tidy. As I work, I remind myself that I am also clearing the rooms of my mind.

My heart is my home.

I continually
clear the clutter
of my life.

HOUSEKEEPING

I make housework fun. I begin anywhere and move through the rooms with artistic flair. I toss out the garbage. I dust and polish those things I treasure. We all have a set of beliefs. And just like a comfortable, familiar reading chair, we keep sitting in these beliefs over and over and over again. I know that my beliefs create my experiences, and some of these create wonderful ones. Others can become like an uncomfortable old chair that I don't want to throw out. I know that I really *can* toss out old beliefs, and I can choose new ones that significantly improve the quality of my life. It's like housecleaning. I need to clean my physical house periodically; otherwise it gets to a point where I really can't live in it. I don't have to be fanatical, but I *do* need to clean. Physically and mentally, I fill the rooms of my house with love.

Simple household chores are a snap for me.

I love to

laugh.

HUMOR

The subconscious mind has no sense of humor. If I make a negative joke about myself or put myself down and just think, *Oh, it doesn't mean anything*, I'm only kidding myself. My subconscious mind still accepts it as true and creates situations accordingly. If I tell put-downs or inappropriate jokes about others, I am still under the law of "What I give out will come back to me." So I have learned to use my humor lovingly and wisely. There is so much humor in life that it is not necessary to denigrate another person or group. Even in humor, we are working to help make the world a more loving and safe place to be.

I use my humor wisely.

$\mathcal{I}$ share my resources and knowledge with those on my path.

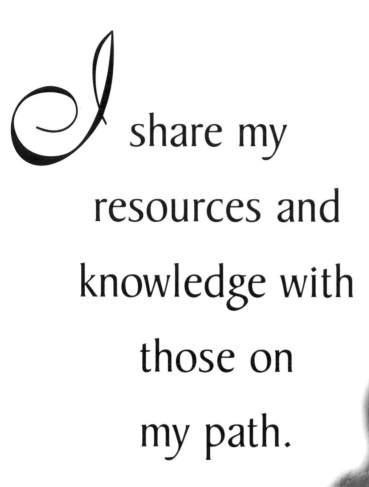

HUNGER

I see old doors closing on hunger, poverty, and suffering, and I see new doors opening on the fair distribution of all resources. There is an incredible abundance on this planet, and literally enough food to feed everyone, yet people are starving. The problem is not a lack of food. It is a lack of love. It is a consciousness that believes in lack, plus people who feel that they do not deserve good in their lives. We must help to raise the consciousness of all people on the planet. To feed someone once is good, but they will be hungry again tomorrow. To paraphrase that old saying, teaching a person how to fish will enable them to feed themselves for the rest of their lives.

There is enough for everyone.

*M*y thoughts support and strengthen my immune system.

IMMUNE SYSTEM

Every day it is getting easier and easier to give myself a good dose of unconditional love. I believe that what I "pick up" depends on where I am in consciousness. Do I believe that "life is hard and I always get the short end of the stick," or "I'm no good anyway, so what difference does it make"? If my beliefs run along these lines, then my immune system (which registers my thoughts and feelings) will be lowered and open to whatever "bug" or "germ" is around at the time. However, if I believe that "life is a joy, and I am lovable and my needs are always met," then my immune system will feel supported, and my body will more easily fight off dis-ease.

My body is intelligent.

IMPROVEMENT

I am a simple human being with an amazingly complex structure of beliefs. I am learning how to get to the love behind the appearances in each of my personal issues. I am kind and patient with myself as I learn and grow and change. Life seems to flow much easier when I make peace with myself on an inner level. It is important to know that I can make changes without seeing myself as a bad person. For too long I have felt I had to be wrong or bad in order to make a change. I thought it was essential in order to make a change, but it is not. It just makes changing very difficult. When I come from loving acceptance, then the positive changes I desire come to me so much easier. Improvement, after all, is natural.

Every day I learn one new idea that will improve the quality of my life.

$\mathcal{M}$y increasing financial status reflects my changing beliefs about income.

INCOME

My income is perfect for me. Every day I love myself a little more, and as I do, I find that I am open to new avenues of income. Prosperity comes through many forms and channels. It is not limited. Some people limit their incomes by saying that they live on a fixed income. But who fixed it? Some people feel that they do not deserve to earn more than their father earned or to go beyond their parents' worthiness level. Well, I can love my parents and still go beyond their income level. There is One Infinite Universe, and out of it comes all the income that everyone makes. The income I am presently making reflects my beliefs and my deservability. It has nothing to do with *getting*. It is really allowing myself to accept. I accept a healthy flow of income for myself.

I bless my income with love and watch it grow.

$\mathcal{I}$ am an individual

expression of Life.

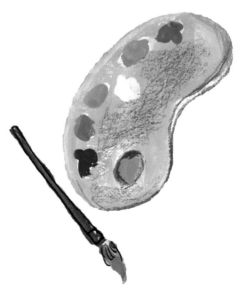

INDIVIDUALITY

I follow my inner star, and sparkle and shine in my own unique way. I am a very precious being. I have a beautiful soul, outer body, and personality. But my soul is the center. My soul is the part of me that is eternal. It always has been and always will be. My soul has taken on many personalities, and it will take on many more. My soul cannot be hurt or destroyed. It can only be enriched by whatever its life experiences are. There is so much more to life than I can possibly comprehend. I shall never know all the answers. But the more I allow myself to understand how life works, the more power and force I have available to me.

I am a light in the world.

choose to

make lessons

easy and fun.

LESSONS

*E*ach one of us is here to learn lessons. When we learn one, we move on to the next. Love is always hidden inside every lesson. I am learning about the relationship between my thoughts and my experiences, and I am doing the best I can with the knowledge and understanding I have. Learning "the lesson" has to do with being willing to change. My higher, spiritual self is changeless and eternal, and so all that really changes is my temporary, human self. I choose to believe that it is easy to make changes. I can resist, deny, get angry, or build walls, but eventually I will learn the lesson anyway. It helps to be willing to learn.

I am willing to learn.

When one door
closes, another
one opens.

LOSS

*N*ature abhors a vacuum. When one thing leaves my life, then something else will come to take its place. Even the loss of a job or a relationship can be a signal that something far greater is coming to take its place. Instead of going into fear or becoming bitter, I open my heart, and I open my arms wide, and I say, "Even better things are coming. I trust Life to take care of me, and I am safe." Then I pay attention to the good in my life.

New and wonderful experiences now enter my life.

$\mathcal{I}$ rejoice in the

love I have to share.

*D*eep at the center of my being, there is an infinite supply of love. It is inexhaustible. I can never use it all in this lifetime. So I do not have to be sparing with it. I can always be generous with my love. Love is contagious. When I share love, it comes back to me multiplied. The more love I give, the more love I have. I have come into this world to be a love giver. I came in full of love. And even though I will share my love all my life, when I leave this earth, I will still have a full and happy heart. If I want more love, then I have only to give. Love is, and I am.

*I am a radiant
being of love.*

I cherish my

meditation times.

MEDITATION

At least once a day I sit quietly, breathe deeply, and go within to connect with that deep, inner, unchanging part of myself. Here resides wisdom and knowledge. Meditating is a joy for me as I connect with my inner place of tranquility. Just sitting quietly with my eyes closed is a way to be deeply relaxed. After a little while, I come back to the present moment refreshed and renewed and ready for the rest of the day. I feel at peace and know that all is well.

The serenity and safety I seek is already within me.

$\mathcal{I}$ love you.

I really love you.

MIRROR TALK

I love you, _____ [insert your own name]. I really, really love you. You are my best friend, and I enjoy living my life with you. Experiences come and go; however, my love for you is constant. We have a good life together, and it will only get better and better. We have many wonderful adventures ahead of us, and a life filled with love and joy. All the love in our lives begins with us. I love you. I really love you.

I talk to you with love.

$\mathcal{I}$n consciousness,

I am always wealthy

and prosperous.

MONEY

oney is merely a means of exchange. It is a form of giving and receiving. As I give to life, life gives me abundance in all its many forms, including money. I affirm that I am always financially secure. Money is my friend, and I attract it easily. I eliminate all thoughts of indebtedness, guilt, and any other negative, poverty-oriented thinking. I pay my way with joy and love, knowing that my income is constantly increasing, and I prosper wherever I turn. I love money, and money loves me.

I am a magnet for money.

*T*hat statement usually makes us feel angry—especially if we're having money worries. Our beliefs about money are so ingrained that it is hard to talk about them without a lot of emotion coming up. It is much easier to teach a workshop on sex than on money. We get very angry when our money patterns are challenged. We want to be aware of how we really feel about money. I could look into a mirror and say to myself, "My biggest worry about money is_____," and then relax and let the feelings come up. Maybe the messages are: "I will never have enough to get out of debt," or "I will be poor like my father," or "I am afraid of becoming a bag lady." If I really believe these thoughts, then it will be impossible for me to attract prosperity. As I become aware of what beliefs are blocking the flow of money in my life, I can choose to change those beliefs. I can begin to create new thoughts. I affirm: *All of my needs are taken care of. I can earn more money than my parents. It is safe for me to be prosperous. I attract abundance now.*

Money is one of the easiest things to demonstrate.

$\mathscr{E}$very moment is a

new beginning for me.

NEW OUTLOOKS

We all do a lot of vacillating between old ideas and new ways of thinking. I am patient with myself through this process. Beating myself up only keeps me stuck. It is better to build myself up instead. Anything I say or think is an affirmation. I become aware of my thoughts and my words. I may discover that a lot of them are very negative. I used to approach life through negative eyes. I would take an ordinary situation like a rainy day, and then say something such as, "Oh, what a terrible day." It was *not* a terrible day; it was a wet day. Just a slight change in the way I look at an event can turn it around. I choose to look at life in a new, positive way.

I enjoy new ways of thinking.

I spread only the good news.

N E W S

We read so much in the news about disasters; there is so much bad news flooding our consciousness. If I read and listen to the news all the time, I am sure to scare myself. I gave up reading the newspapers a long time ago. Any piece of news I am meant to know, someone will tell me. The media wants to sell their products, so they dig up the worst-case scenarios to catch our attention. I would like to see a boycott on all news until the media begins to tell us at least 75 percent good news. This would encourage us all to see life in a more positive way. We could begin by writing to the papers, magazines, and TV stations, requesting more good news. Together, we can envision positive news happening, and we can hear the cry for love that is hidden in every negative report.

I envision positive news reports.

I lovingly

take charge of

my body now.

NUTRITION

I care enough for my body to nourish myself with all the best that life has to offer. I learn about nutrition because I am a precious being, and I want to take the best care of myself that I can. My body is special—different from all other bodies; therefore, I learn the things my body assimilates the best. I learn everything I can about food and beverages. I pay attention to what I eat and drink, and I notice if some food or beverage does not seem to agree with me. If I have something to eat and an hour later I fall asleep, I realize that that particular food is not good for my body at this time. I search out the foods that renew my cells and give me good energy. I bless all my food with love and gratitude. I am nurtured and nourished. I feel healthy, happy, and energized.

I nourish myself each and every day.

I approve of myself

I ask my mother to make a cassette tape telling me how wonderful I am.

148

OLD TAPES

Old tapes of my childhood used to run my life. Most people have about 25,000 hours of parent tapes running through their minds. Many of these old tapes had a lot of negative messages in them, lots of criticism and "shoulds" . . . and not enough "I love you and you are wonderful and wanted." Now I am choosing to erase them and to create new, positive messages. I listen to my inner thoughts, and when I catch one that makes me feel uncomfortable, I turn it around. I do not have to obediently listen to the old stuff. I can just re-create. I know I am a capable person. I know I am worth loving. I really believe I am worthy of a wonderful life. I have a purpose in being here. I have the power to change the old tapes. Those old negative messages are not the truth of my being.

I live in the Now.

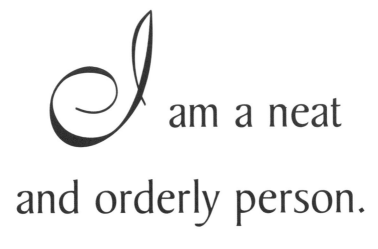

I am a neat
and orderly person.

ORDER

*I*t gives me pleasure to arrange my things in such a way that when I am looking for them, I can easily find them. Everything is in Divine right order, from the stars in the heavens to the clothes in my closet and the papers on my desk. I love the ceremony of my daily routines, which exercise my body and train my mind. It seems that when my life is in order, I have the time to be creative and open to new insights. And still, my routines are flexible, fun, and effective in helping me do what I came here to do. I am part of the Divine plan. All is in perfect order in my world.

*Everything I need
is at hand.*

$\mathcal{L}$ove will always

dissolve pain.

PAIN

My Higher Self shows me the way to live a pain-free life, both emotionally and physically. I am learning to respond to pain as if it were an alarm clock signaling me to wake up to my inner wisdom. Something I am thinking or doing is not for my highest good. Am I angry at myself or my body? Healing begins with love for myself and love for every part of my body. As I move in consciousness from anger or fear to love, my situations and my health move in a positive direction. I love my body, and I love my mind, and I am thankful that they are so closely related.

Loving my body is the first step in healing.

$\mathcal{M}_y$

parents are

wonderful people.

PARENTS

*N*ow is the time for me to stand up on my own two feet, to support myself, to think for myself, to give myself what my parents could not give me. The more I learn about their childhoods, the more I understand their limitations. No one taught them how to be parents. They were living out the limitations that their own parents had. Parent issues are something that we all deal with every day. The best we can do is to love and accept them as they are, and affirm that they love and accept us as we are. I do not use my parents as an excuse for the negative parts of my life. I bless my parents with love, and we are all free to accept happiness that is meaningful to us.

*My parents, too,
were once children.*

All is well.
Everything I need
comes to me at
the perfect
moment.

PATIENCE

When I am impatient, I know it is because I do not want to take the time to learn the lesson at hand. I want it done now. Or, as I once heard: "Instant gratification is not soon enough." There is always something to learn, something to know. Patience is being at peace with the process of life, knowing that everything happens in the perfect time/space sequence. If I am not having completion now, then there is something more for me to know. Being impatient does not speed up the process; it only wastes time. So I breathe deeply, go within, and ask, "What do I need to know?" Then I patiently wait to receive the help that is all around me.

I have plenty of time.

$\mathcal{I}$ choose

a serene way

of life.

PEACE

If I want to live in a peaceful world, then it is up to me to make sure that I am a peaceful person. No matter how others behave, I keep peace in my heart. I declare peace in the midst of chaos or madness. I surround all difficult situations with peace and love. I send thoughts of peace to all troubled parts of the world. If I want the world to change for the better, then I need to change the way I see the world. I am now willing to see life in a very positive way. I know that peace begins with my own thoughts. As I choose peaceful thoughts, I am connected with like-minded, peaceful-thinking people. Together we will help bring peace and loving kindness to our world.

Peace begins with me.

$\mathcal{I}$ am perfect,
whole, and complete.

PERFECTION

*N*o little baby ever says, "Oh, my hips are too big," or "My nose is too long." Babies know how perfect they are, and once we were all like that. We accepted our perfection as normal and natural. As we grew up, we began to doubt our perfection, and we tried to become perfect. We cannot become what we already are. We can only accept it. There is nothing wrong with us. So let us once again affirm and know that we are Divine, magnificent expressions of Life and that, really, all is well in our world.

I am completely happy with myself—body and soul.

My life is in order at a very deep, peaceful level.

PERFECT ORDER

The stars, the moon, and the sun are all operating in perfect Divine right order. There is an order, a rhythm, and a purpose to their pathways. I am part of the Universe; therefore, I know that there is an order, a rhythm, and a purpose to my life. Sometimes my life may seem to be in chaos, and yet, in back of the chaos, I know that there is a Divine order. As I put my mind in order by choosing positive thoughts, the chaos disappears, and the order comes back. I trust that my life is really in perfect Divine right order. All is well in my world.

The Universe is in perfect order.

I see Earth as being healed and whole, with everyone fed, clothed, housed, and happy.

PLANETARY HEALING

There is so much good I can do for the planet on an individual level. At times, I may work for causes, putting my physical energy or finances into them. At other times, I may use the power of my thoughts to help heal the planet. If I hear news of a world disaster or acts of senseless violence, I immediately surround the entire situation with love and affirm that out of this experience, only good will come. I send positive energy and do visualizations, seeing the incident working out with a solution that is best for everyone. I bless the perpetrators with love and affirm that the part of them where love and compassion dwells comes to the surface and that they, too, are healed. It is only when we are all healed and whole that we will have a healthy world to live in.

I affirm the highest good for everyone on the planet.

I love this marvelous marvelous planet Earth.

PLANET EARTH

The earth is a wise and loving mother. She provides everything we could ever need. There is water, food, air, and companionship. We have an infinite variety of animals, vegetation, birds, fish, and other natural wonders. We have treated this planet very poorly in the last few years, using up our valuable resources. If we continue to disrespect the planet, we will have no place to live. I commit to lovingly taking care of and improving the quality of life in this world. My thoughts are clear and loving and concerned. I express random acts of kindness whenever I can. I recycle, compost, organically garden, and improve the quality of the soil. It is my planet, and I help to make it a better place to live. I imagine a peaceful planet, with a clean, healthy environment for all. I see all the people on the planet opening their hearts and their minds and working together to create a world where it is safe for us to love each other. It is possible, and it begins with me.

I appreciate the beautiful world I live in.

$\mathcal{T}$he point of power is in the present moment.

POWER

I have the power to heal my life, and I need to know that. I am not helpless. I have the power of my own mind. My thoughts create the sort of life I live. I no longer choose to think of myself as a victim, for those are powerless thoughts. I have given up complaining and whining. I choose in this present moment to claim the power of my thoughts and use them wisely. I choose thoughts that make me feel happy. I choose thoughts of gratitude and appreciation for life. I am connected with the One Power and Intelligence that created me. I am supported by Life, and I am loved.

I claim my power now.

We are all one.

PREJUDICE

We all live on the same planet. We walk on the same earth. We breathe the same air. No matter where I was born, no matter what color skin I have or what religion I was raised to believe in, everything and everyone is connected to this one life. I no longer choose to prejudge others, to feel either superior or inferior. I choose equality—to have warm, loving, open communication with every member of my Earthly family. I am a member of the Earth community. Differences of opinion are wonderful, colorful varieties of expression. Today my heart opens a little bit more as I go about creating the world I want to live in.

Love is stronger than differences.

$\mathcal{E}$very problem has a

solution, and this solution

begins in my mind.

PROBLEM SOLVING

No matter what the problem or how big and overwhelming it seems, the place to begin is in the quiet of my mind. I take a big, deep breath and repeat over and over: *"All is well. Everything is working out for my highest good. Out of this situation only good will come, and I am safe!"* This simple affirmation stills the chatter of my mind allows the Universe to find the perfect solution. It has worked miracles in my life.

I am solution oriented.

I have a

prosperity

consciousness.

PROSPERITY

I have inherited a great treasure—the love in my own heart. The more I share this treasure with others, the richer I become. Prosperity begins with feeling good about myself. If I do not feel good about myself, I cannot really enjoy anything. My home, car, clothing, friends, health, and bank account are only reflections of my thoughts about myself and what I believe I deserve. No matter where I am or what is happening, I can change my thoughts and beliefs. True prosperity is never an amount of money; it is a state of mind. My mind is now open to receiving prosperity. Once a day, I stretch my arms out wide and say, "I am open and receptive to all the good and abundance in the Universe. Thank you, Life."

I always have everything I need.

I am here to live

my life with purpose

and meaning.

PURPOSE

Being alive at this time is an incredible opportunity to explore and experience the Universe and myself. In a way, the self is the new frontier. I have come to know my limited self pretty well, and now I am coming to know my unlimited self. My purpose is unfolding each moment as I calm down and know that I am far more than my personality, problems, fears, or dis-eases. I am spirit, light, energy, and love, and I have the power to live my life with meaning and purpose. I am doing the best I can and am constantly discovering new ways to improve the quality of my life. I am so grateful to be here.

My purpose is to learn to love unconditionally.

RELATIONSHIPS

*R*elationships are wonderful, and marriages can be wonderful, but they are all temporary because there comes a time when they end. The one person I am with forever is *me*. My relationship with myself is eternal, so I choose to be my own best friend. I choose to love and accept myself and to talk to myself as I would to a beloved person in my life. I saturate all the cells in my body with love, and they become vibrantly healthy. I know that I am always connected to a Universe that loves me. I draw loving people and loving experiences to me. I relate with love to all of life.

I am creating lots of room for love.

All of my new habits support me in positive ways.

RELEASING HABITS

When I am ready to let go of an old pattern, it comes up as an issue. I am learning to recognize my issues as messengers from a deep place inside myself that yearns to be loved. I ask the Universe to help me let go of the fear, and I allow myself to move into the new understanding. I am learning to be loving to my negative habits and beliefs. I used to say, "Oh, I want to get rid of that." Now I know that I created all my habits to fulfill a purpose. So I release the old habits with love and find more positive ways to fulfill those needs.

I release the need to be perfect.

$\mathcal{M}$y religion

is based on love.

RELIGION

I am steady and secure as I connect with the One Infinite Intelligence, the Eternal Power that created me and everything else in the Universe. I feel this Power within me. Every nerve and cell in my body recognizes this Power as good. The reality of my being is always connected with the Power that created me, regardless of what any religion tells me. As I accept myself and know that I am good enough, I open myself to the healing power of my own love. The love of the Universe surrounds me and dwells within me. I am worthy of this love. Love is now flowing through my life. I have found a concept of God that supports me.

I connect with the Power that created me.

$\mathcal{I}$ let go, and I forgive.

RESENTMENT

*B*abies express their anger freely. As we grow up, we learn to stuff our anger, and it turns into resentment. It lodges in our bodies, eating away at us. In years past, like many people, I used to live in a prison of self-righteous resentment. I felt that I had the right to be angry because of all the things "they" did to me. It took me a long time to learn that holding on to bitterness and resentment did me more harm than the original incident. When I refused to forgive, *I* was the person who was hurting. The door to my heart was sealed, and I could not love. I learned that forgiveness did not mean that I condoned another person's negative behavior. Releasing my resentment let me out of prison. The door to my heart opened, and I found that I was free. I forgive, I let go, and I fly free.

I release the need to dwell in resentment.

$\mathcal{I}$ am the responsible

power in my life.

RESPONSIBILITY

When we first hear that we are responsible for our experiences, we think we are being blamed. And blame makes us feel guilty and wrong. However, there is no blame involved. To understand that we are responsible is to be given a great gift, for the same power that helps to create experiences can also change them. We go from being powerless over our circumstances to being people who can mold and shape our lives in positive ways. As we learn to use our thoughts in productive ways, we become powerful people. It gives us the power to respond to life, to make changes, and to improve the quality of our lives.

I accept my responsibilities with ease.

I have high

self-esteem,

and I am safe.

SAFE SEX

Women have had the complete burden of safe sex for hundreds, if not thousands, of years. If women did not practice safe sex, then they were open to contracting infectious dis-eases, as well as to getting pregnant. Now, men—particularly gay men—are beginning to understand what the responsibility of safe sex entails. When the body is in the heat of passion, it does not want to listen to the mind giving it careful instructions of safety. What do I say to someone who refuses to wear a condom? The answer always has to do with my own level of self-esteem. If my self-love and self-esteem are high, I will refuse to have sex that is not safe. If I do not think very much of myself, I will probably "give in" and hope it will be all right. So how much do I love myself? How much will I allow myself to be abused? It will be less and less as my love for myself grows. People who love themselves will not abuse themselves or others.

I love myself enough to refuse to have sex that is not safe.

$\mathcal{L}$ove makes
my world go
'round.

I treat myself as if I am someone who is deeply loved. All kinds of events come and go; yet, through it all, my love for myself is constant. This is not being vain or conceited. People who are vain or conceited have a lot of self-hatred covered over by a layer of "I'm better than you." Self-love is simply appreciating the miracle of my own being. When I really love myself, I cannot hurt myself, and I cannot hurt another person. To me, the answer to world peace is unconditional love. It begins with self-acceptance and self-love. I no longer wait to be perfect in order to love myself. I accept myself exactly as I am, right here and now.

My love is powerful.

I love

my own

thoughts.

SELF-TALK

I have a unique role to play on this earth, and I also have the tools to do the job. The thoughts I think and the words I speak are my incredibly powerful tools. I use them and I enjoy what they produce for me. Meditation, prayer, or ten minutes of affirmations in the morning are wonderful. And I get even better results when I am consistent all day long. I remember that it is the moment-to-moment thinking that is really shaping my life. The point of power, the place where I make changes, is always right here and now. So, just for the moment, I catch the thought I am thinking right now. And I ask myself, "Do I want that thought to create my future?" I can always choose a more loving thought.

My inner dialogue is kind and loving.

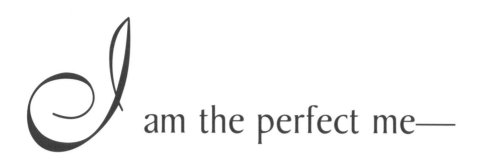

I am the perfect me—

physically, sexually,

mentally, and spiritually.

SEXUALITY

I believe that before we are born into each lifetime, we choose our country, our color, our sexuality, and the perfect set of parents to match the patterns that we have chosen to work on in this lifetime. Each lifetime, I seem to choose a different type of sexuality. Sometimes I am a man; sometimes I am a woman. Sometimes I am heterosexual; sometimes I am homosexual. Each form of sexuality has its own areas of fulfillment and challenges. Sometimes society approves of my sexuality, and sometimes it does not. Yet, at all times, I am me—perfect, whole, and complete. My soul has no sexuality. It is only my personality that does. I love and cherish every part of my body, including my genitals. I am at peace with my body.

I accept and am happy with my sexuality.

When I am ready, my spiritual growth unfolds in wondrous ways.

SPIRITUAL GROWTH

My spiritual growth often comes to me in strange ways. It can be a chance meeting, an accident, a dis-ease, or the loss of a loved one. Something inside urges me to follow a certain path, or I am forcefully prevented from living in the same old way. It is a little different for each person. I grow spiritually when I accept responsibility for my life. This gives me the inner power to make the changes in myself that I need to make. Spiritual growth is not about changing others. Spiritual growth happens to the person who is ready to step out of the victim role, into forgiveness, and into a new life. None of this happens overnight. It is an unfolding process. Loving myself opens the door, and being willing to change really helps.

I am willing to change and grow.

When I learn the Spiritual Laws of life, "magic" is demonstrated in my life.

SPIRITUAL LAWS

I am protected by the best insurance plan under the sun: knowledge of Spiritual Laws and a love of working with them in all areas of my life. Learning Spiritual Laws is very much like learning to operate a computer or VCR. When I calm down and slowly and patiently learn the step-by-step procedures of the computer, it works beautifully. It is almost like magic. If I do not do my homework and do not follow the computer's laws to the letter, then either nothing happens or it will not work the way I want it to. The computer will not give an inch. I can get as frustrated as I want while it patiently waits for me to learn its laws, and then it gives me magic. It takes practice. And it is the same with learning the Spiritual Laws of life.

The Laws of Energy are always operating.

I consciously connect with my subconscious mind.

SUBCONSCIOUS MIND

*M*y subconscious mind is a storehouse of information. It records everything I think and say. If I put a negative in, then I get a negative out. When I put a positive in, I get a positive out. My subconscious mind will produce whatever I feed it. Therefore, I consciously choose to feed it positive, loving, and uplifting messages that produce beneficial experiences for me. I now release any thought, idea, or belief that limits me. I reprogram my subconscious mind with new beliefs that create the most wonderful, prosperous, joyous events in my life.

I program my subconscious mind with loving messages.

*T*o succeed, I must
believe the thought that
I am a success, rather than
thinking I am a failure.

SUCCESS

*J*ust like the acorn has the complete oak tree within its tiny form, so do I have success within me. I take tiny steps from where I am right now, and I dream big. I encourage and praise my improvements. I learn from every experience, and it is okay for me to make mistakes while I am learning. This way I move from success to success, and every day it gets easier to see things in this light. I realize that failure is a learning lesson, and I give it no power. There is only one Power in this entire Universe, and this Power is 100 percent successful in everything It does. It created me; therefore, I am already a beautiful, successful person.

I have within me all of the ingredients for success.

 relax, and

know that Life

supports me at

all times.

I am neither lonely nor lost nor abandoned in the Universe. All of Life supports me every moment of the day and night. Everything I need for a fulfilling life is already provided for me. There is enough breath to last me for as long as I shall live. The earth is supplied with an abundance of food. There are millions of people to interact with. I am supported in every possible way. Every thought I think is mirrored for me in my experiences. Life always says yes to me. All I need to do is accept this abundance and support with joy, pleasure, and gratitude. I now release from within my consciousness any and all patterns or beliefs that would deny me my good. I am loved and supported by Life itself.

I am supported by Life.

We make

quantum leaps in

consciousness together.

SUPPORT GROUPS

The new social norm is "support groups." There are support groups for any problem that we, as individuals, may have. We have self-help groups, personal growth groups, spiritual groups, and 12-step programs. These support groups are much more beneficial than sitting at home and whining. We learn we do not have to struggle by ourselves, and we do not have to stay stuck in our patterns. We can reach out to a group of people with the same issues, and we can work together to find positive solutions. We care for and support each other as we learn to leave the pain of the past behind. We do not sit in self-pity, bemoaning our past and playing "Ain't It Awful." We find ways to forgive and get on with our lives. We support each other, and we heal together.

*There is help
wherever we turn.*

$\mathscr{M}$y doctors are

pleased that I am

healing so quickly.

SURGERY

Whenever I need a doctor or health-care professional, I am always drawn to one with healing hands, a positive attitude, and a loving heart. We work together as a healing team. I know that the wisdom of the Universe works through the medical profession, so I relax and accept its gentle, caring attention as I move through this experience. Every hand that touches my body is a healing hand, and I know that the real healing is within me. My body is always working toward perfect health. I trust my body to get well. I am healthy, healed, and whole.

It is safe for me to get well.

Life loves me, and I am safe.

TEENAGERS

*I*t is safe for me to grow up. I love to learn, grow, and change, and I feel safe in the midst of it all, knowing that change is a natural part of life. My personality is flexible, and it is easy for me to go with the flow of life. My inner being is consistent; therefore, I am safe in every kind of experience. When I was a little child, I did not know what the future would bring. As I now begin my journey into adulthood, I realize that tomorrow is equally unknown and mysterious. I choose to believe that it is safe for me to grow up and take charge of my life. My first adult act is to learn to love myself unconditionally, for then I can handle whatever the future may bring.

I feel safe as I make my journey toward adulthood.

 thoughts

weave the tapestry

of my life.

THOUGHTS

I used to fear my thoughts, for they made me so uncomfortable. I thought I had no control over them. Then I learned that my thinking was creating my experiences and that I could choose to think any thought I wanted to. As I learned to take control of my thoughts and gently channel them in the directions I wanted them to go, my entire life began to change for the better. Now I know that I am the thinker that chooses my thoughts. If a negative thought pops up, I let it pass like a cloud on a summer day. I choose to release thoughts of resentment, shame, and guilt. I choose to think thoughts of love, peace, and joy—as well as ways in which I can help heal the planet. My thoughts have become my friends, and I enjoy choosing fun ones to think.

*My thoughts
are my best friends.*

TIME

ime is exactly what I make it to be. If I choose to feel rushed, then time speeds up and I do not have enough of it. If I choose to believe that there is always enough time for me to do the things I want to do, then time slows down and I accomplish what I set out to do. If I find myself stuck in traffic, I immediately affirm that all of us drivers are doing our best to get there as soon as we can, and I will get to my destination at the perfect time. When I see the perfection of each experience, then I am never hurried or delayed. I am always in the right place at the right time, and all is well.

I always arrive at the right place at the right time.

 am in the

most wonderful

time of transition.

TRANSITION

I am living in a time of change. It is a time of releasing old, limiting beliefs and learning new ways of thinking. Loneliness, anger, fear, and pain are all part of the old fear syndrome, and that is what I choose to change. I choose to move from fear into love. I am learning to go within, and I find that I have the power to change myself and my world. I no longer need to be a victim. I can choose thoughts and beliefs that lead to freedom. I have learned to take responsibility for my life and to respond in ways that empower me and make positive changes in my life.

I am willing to change.

$\mathcal{I}$ put love
into all my trips.
Everywhere I go,
love is waiting
for me.

*N*o matter what form of transportation I use, I know that I am safe and Divinely protected. Airplanes, automobiles, bicycles, boats, buses, scooters, skateboards, and trucks are all safe means of moving from place to place. If I find myself holding my breath or becoming tense, I relax my shoulders, breathe deeply, and affirm my connection with Life. I know that Life loves me and wants me to have a good time wherever I go.

*I am a
peaceful traveler.*

trust that Life will

provide me with everything

I need and want.

TRUST

I know that I was born a beautiful and trusting soul. If things get difficult, I turn within and anchor my thoughts in truth and love. I ask for guidance from the Universe, and I make my way safely through stormy seas and calm, blissful weather. My job is to stay in the present moment and to choose clear, simple, positive thoughts and words. I trust the process of Life in all its mysterious and wondrous ways.

*I trust myself,
and I trust Life.*

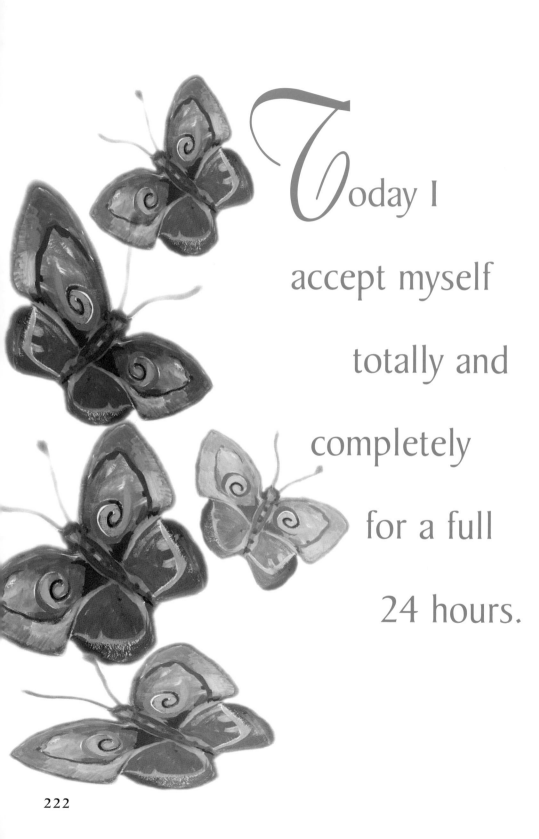

*T*oday I accept myself totally and completely for a full 24 hours.

UNCONDITIONAL LOVE

*A*s I love and accept myself exactly as I am, right here and right now with all my so-called flaws and imperfections, I find it easier to accept others in the same way. When I put conditions on my love, for myself or others, then I am not loving freely. "I will love you if" is not love; it is control. I am learning to release the need to control others and allow them the freedom to be who they are. I am learning to create peace within, and am doing the best I can with the understanding, knowledge, and awareness that I have at this time. As I open my consciousness to tap in to unconditional love, I connect with new levels of spiritual power. I see a blanket of benevolence covering the planet, helping to transform Earth's consciousness from fear to love.

The love I give is the love I receive.

The more I
understand about life,
the more my
world expands.

UNDERSTANDING

I am teachable. Every day I open my awareness a little more to the Divine Wisdom within me. I am glad to be alive, and I am so grateful for the good that has come into my life. To me, life is an education. Every day I open my mind and my heart, as a child does, and I discover new insights, new people, new viewpoints, and new ways to understand the process of life and how things work. My expanding understanding is helping me feel more at ease with all the changes in this incredible school of life here on Planet Earth.

I am constantly increasing my understanding.

n uniqueness,

there is no

competition

and no

comparison.

UNIQUENESS

We are all one in Spirit. Yet, our faces and bodies are quite different and so are our personalities. We are unique and different expressions of the one Life. There has never been anyone like me before, and I rejoice in my uniqueness. I am neither too much nor too little, and I do not have to prove myself to anyone. I choose to cherish and love myself as the Divine, magnificent expression of Life that I am. Being me is an exhilarating adventure! I follow my inner star, and sparkle and shine in my own unique way. I love life, and I love me!

I am unique,
and so is everyone else.

VISION

I have clarity of vision and purpose. My inner knowing always directs me in ways that arc for my highest good and greatest joy. I connect with the infinity of Life where all is perfect, whole, and complete. In the midst of ever-changing life, I am centered. I begin to see the good in everyone and everything.

I see clearly now.

I trust my inner wisdom.

WISDOM

Deep at the center of my being, there is a well of inner wisdom. All the answers to all the questions I shall ever ask reside there. This inner wisdom is connected to the vast wisdom of the Universe, so I am never at a loss for answers. Every day is a joyous new adventure for me because I choose to listen to my own inner wisdom. This wisdom is always available to me. It comes through the essence of my being. I ask and I receive. And I am grateful.

Inner wisdom guides me at all times.

About the Author

Louise L. Hay is a metaphysical lecturer and teacher and the bestselling author of 27 books, including *You Can Heal Your Life* and *Empowering Women*. Her works have been translated into 25 different languages in 33 countries throughout the world. Since beginning her career as a Science of Mind minister in 1981, Louise has assisted thousands of people in discovering and using the full potential of their own creative powers for personal growth and self-healing. Louise is the founder and chairman of Hay House, Inc., a publishing company that disseminates books, audios, and videos that contribute to the healing of the planet.

Other Hay House Lifestyles Titles of Related Interest

Books

Dream Journal, by Leon Nacson

Dr. Wayne Dyer's 10 Secrets for Success and Inner Peace,
by Dr. Wayne W. Dyer

Interpreting Dreams A–Z, by Leon Nacson

A Journal of Love and Healing,
by Sylvia Browne and Nancy Dufresne

The Love and Power Journal, by Lynn V. Andrews

Meditations, by Sylvia Browne

Pleasant Dreams, by Amy E. Dean

Prayers, by Sylvia Browne

Simple Things, by Jim Brickman

Card Decks

Feng Shui Personal Paradise Cards
(booklet and card deck), by Terah Kathryn Collins

The Four Agreements Cards, by DON Miguel Ruiz

Healthy Body Cards, by Louise L. Hay

Heart and Soul, by Sylvia Browne

Inner Peace Cards, by Dr. Wayne W. Dyer

MarsVenus Cards, by John Gray

Messages from Your Angels Oracle Cards,
by Doreen Virtue, Ph.D.

Miracle Cards, by Marianne Williamson

Self-Care Cards, by Cheryl Richardson

Wisdom Cards, by Louise L. Hay

Zen Cards, by Daniel Levin

೦೦ ೦೦ ೦೦

All of the above titles are available at your
local bookstore, or may be ordered by calling
Hay House at (800) 654-5126.

೦೦ ೦೦ ೦೦

✺ ✺ ✺

We hope you enjoyed this Hay House Lifestyles book.
For a free catalog of books, audios, videos, and other
products by Louise L. Hay and other Hay House
authors—and/or to receive a free premier issue of
The Louise Hay Newsletter—please contact:

Hay House, Inc.
P.O. Box 5100
Carlsbad, CA 92018-5100

(760) 431-7695 or **(800) 654-5126**
(760) 431-6948 (fax) or **(800) 650-5115 (fax)**

✺✺✺

Hay House Australia Pty Ltd
P.O. Box 515
Brighton-Le-Sands, NSW 2216
phone: 1800 023 516
e-mail: info@hayhouse.com.au

✺✺✺

Please visit the Hay House Website at: **hayhouse.com**

✺ ✺ ✺